THANKSGIVING
COLORING BOOK

SIMPLE BIG PICTURES HAPPY HOLIDAY COLORING BOOKS FOR TODDLERS AND PRESCHOOLERS

The Coloring Book Art Design Studio

THANKSGIVING COLORING BOOK

by The Coloring Book Art Design Studio

THANKSGIVING COLORING BOOK

THIS BOOK
BELONG TO

____

____

LET'S TEST YOUR COLOR

AUTUMN FESTIVAL
HAPPY
Thanksgiving

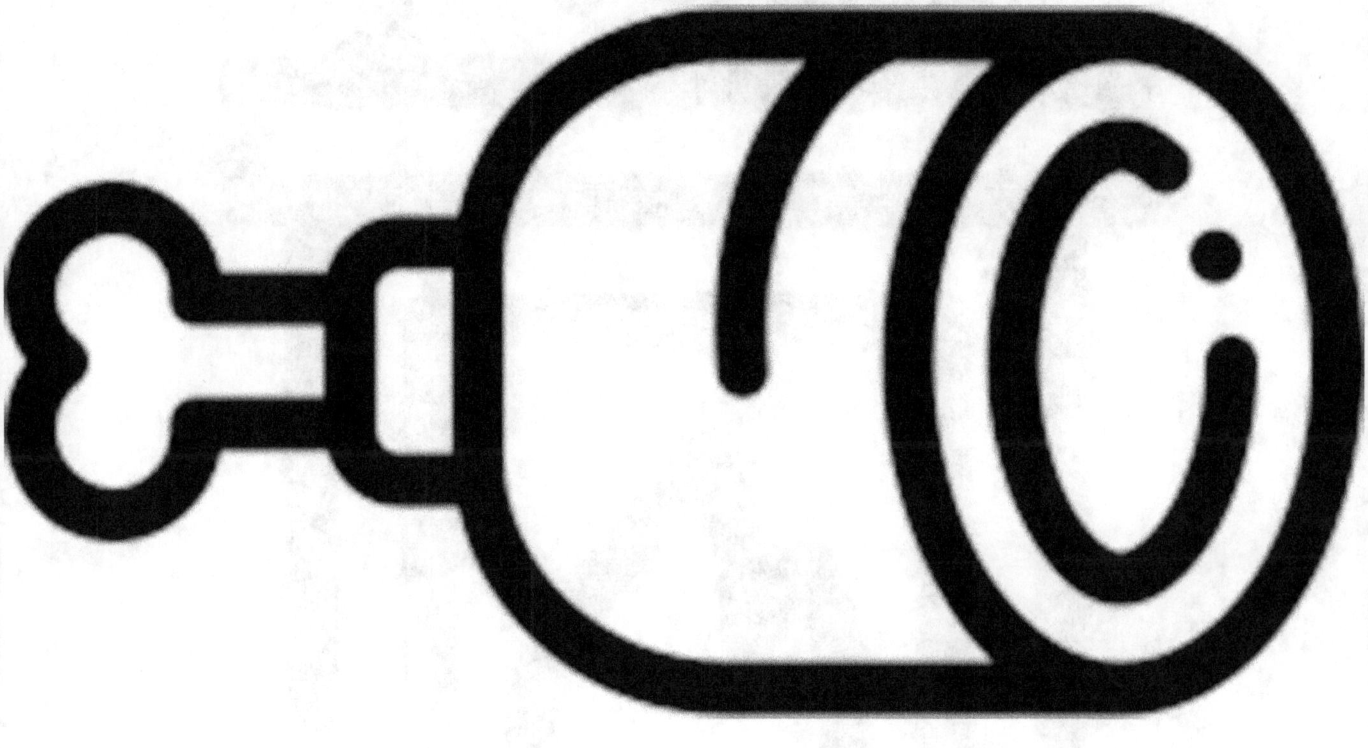

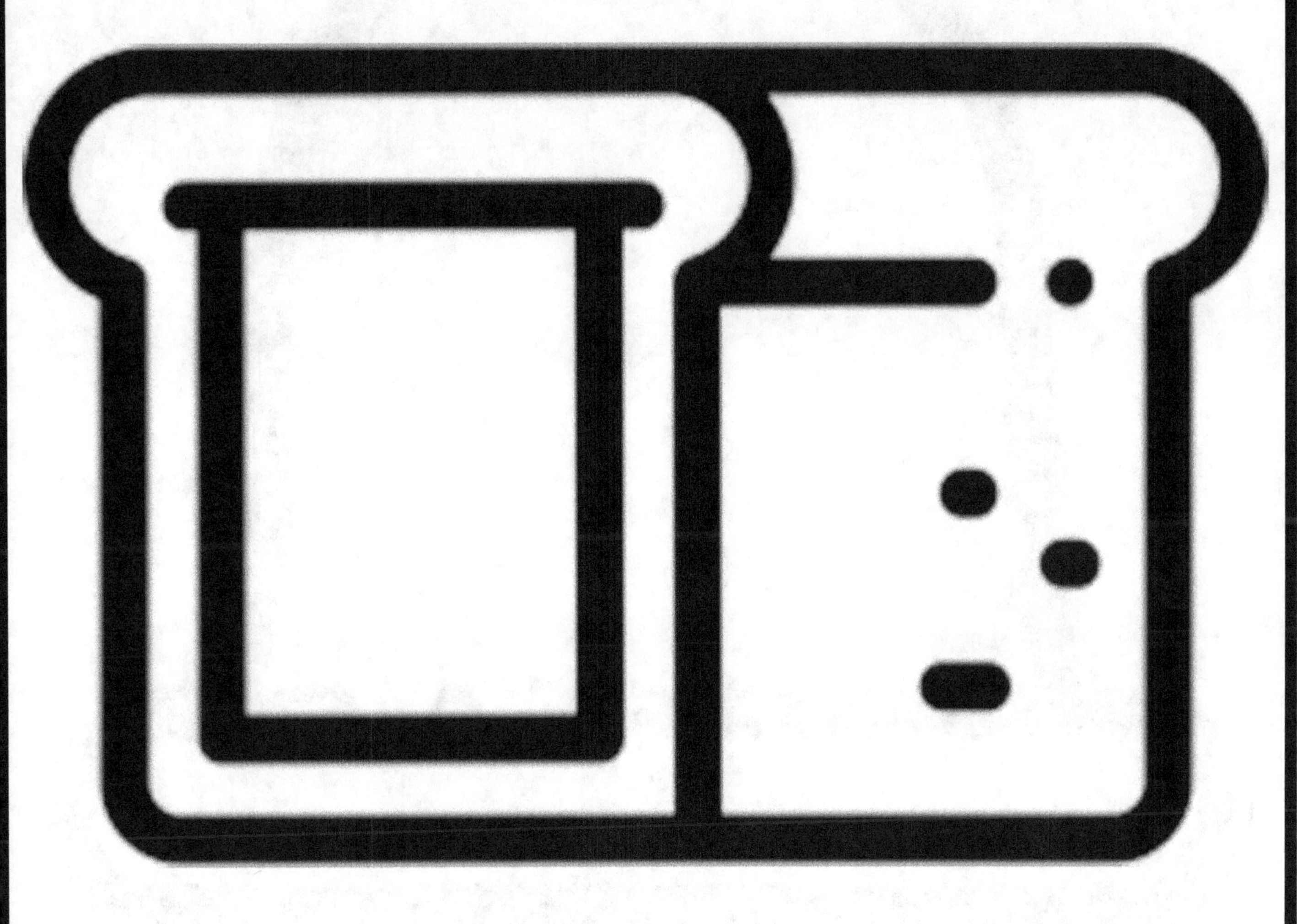

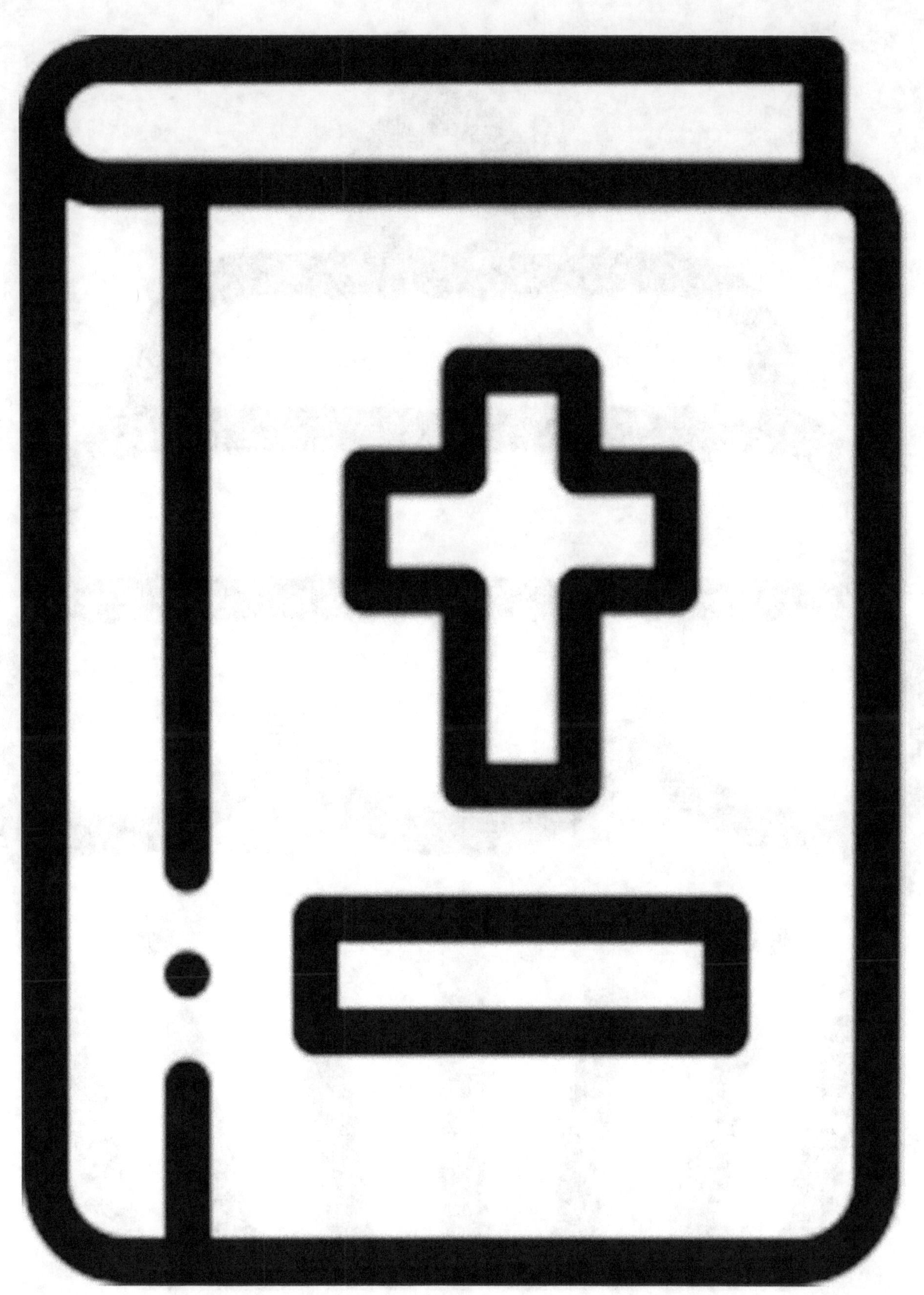

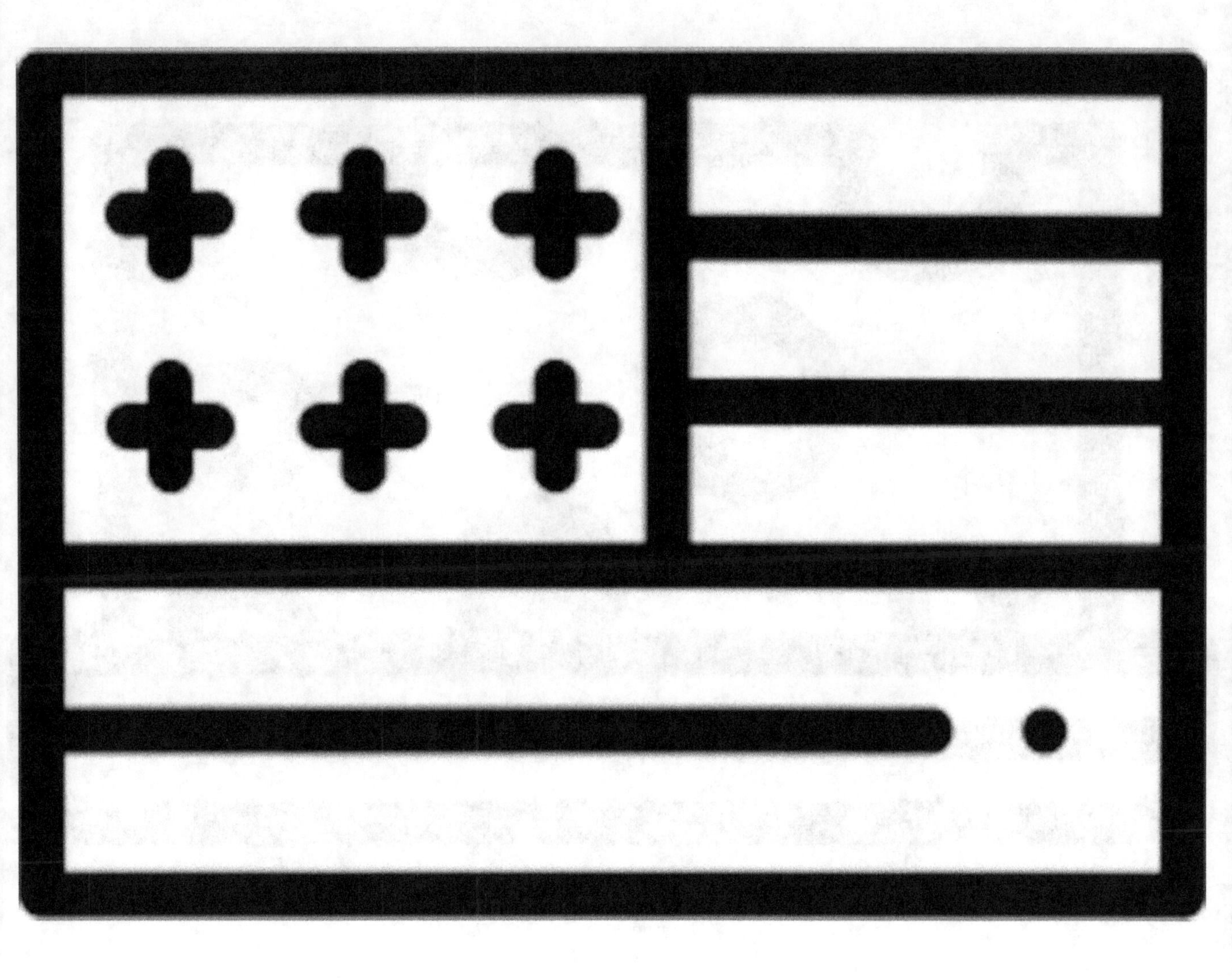

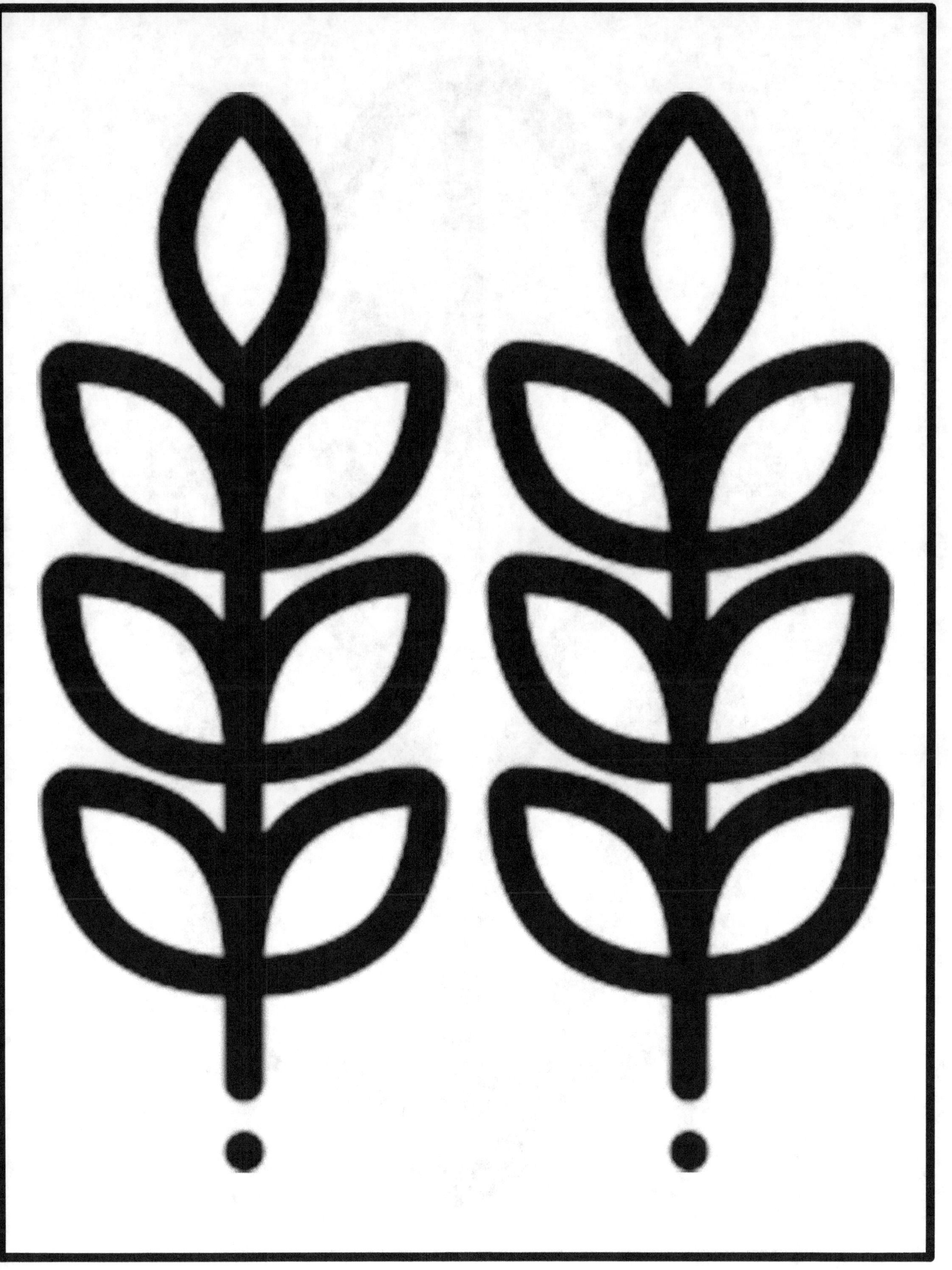

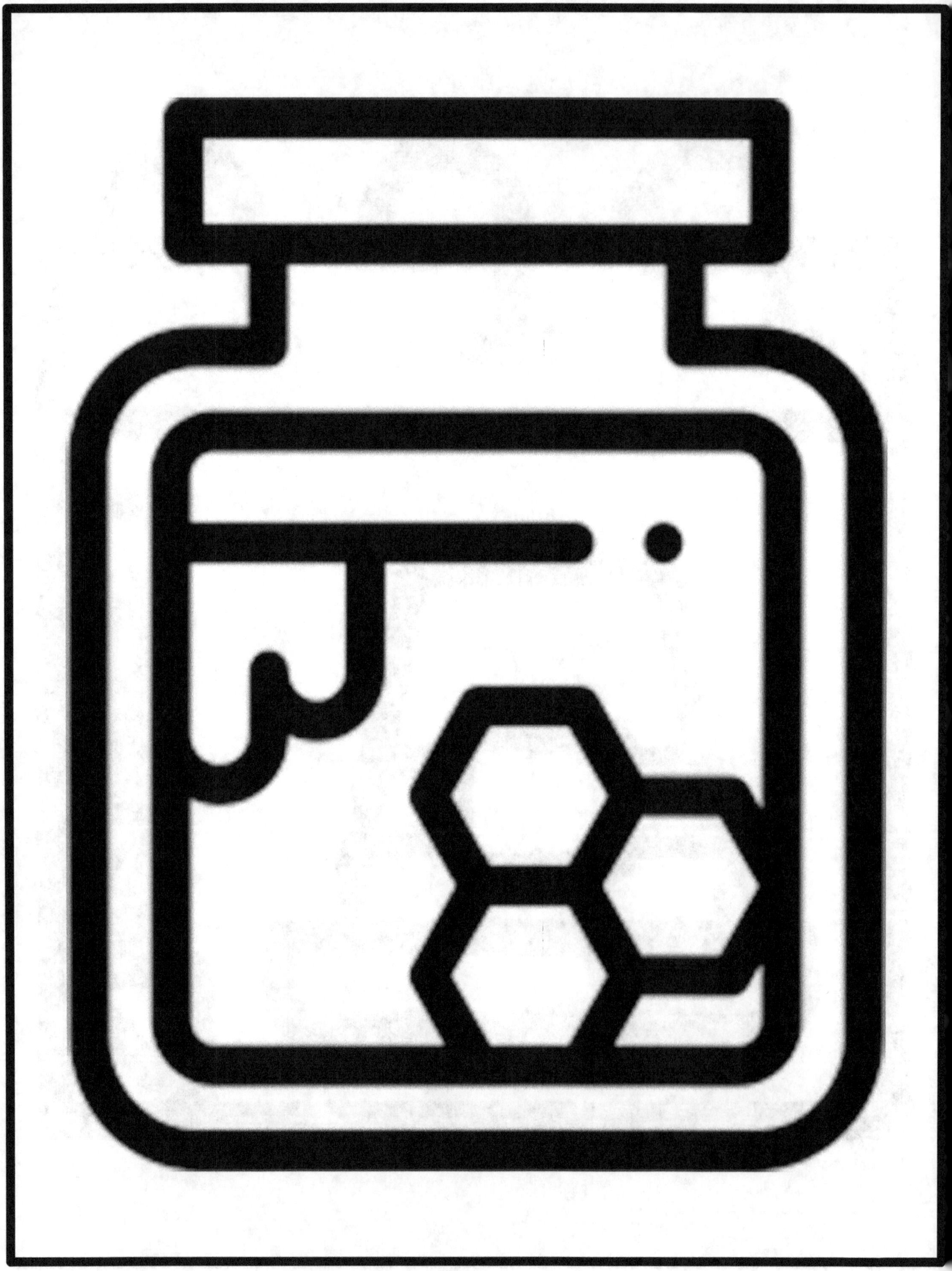

Thank
you!

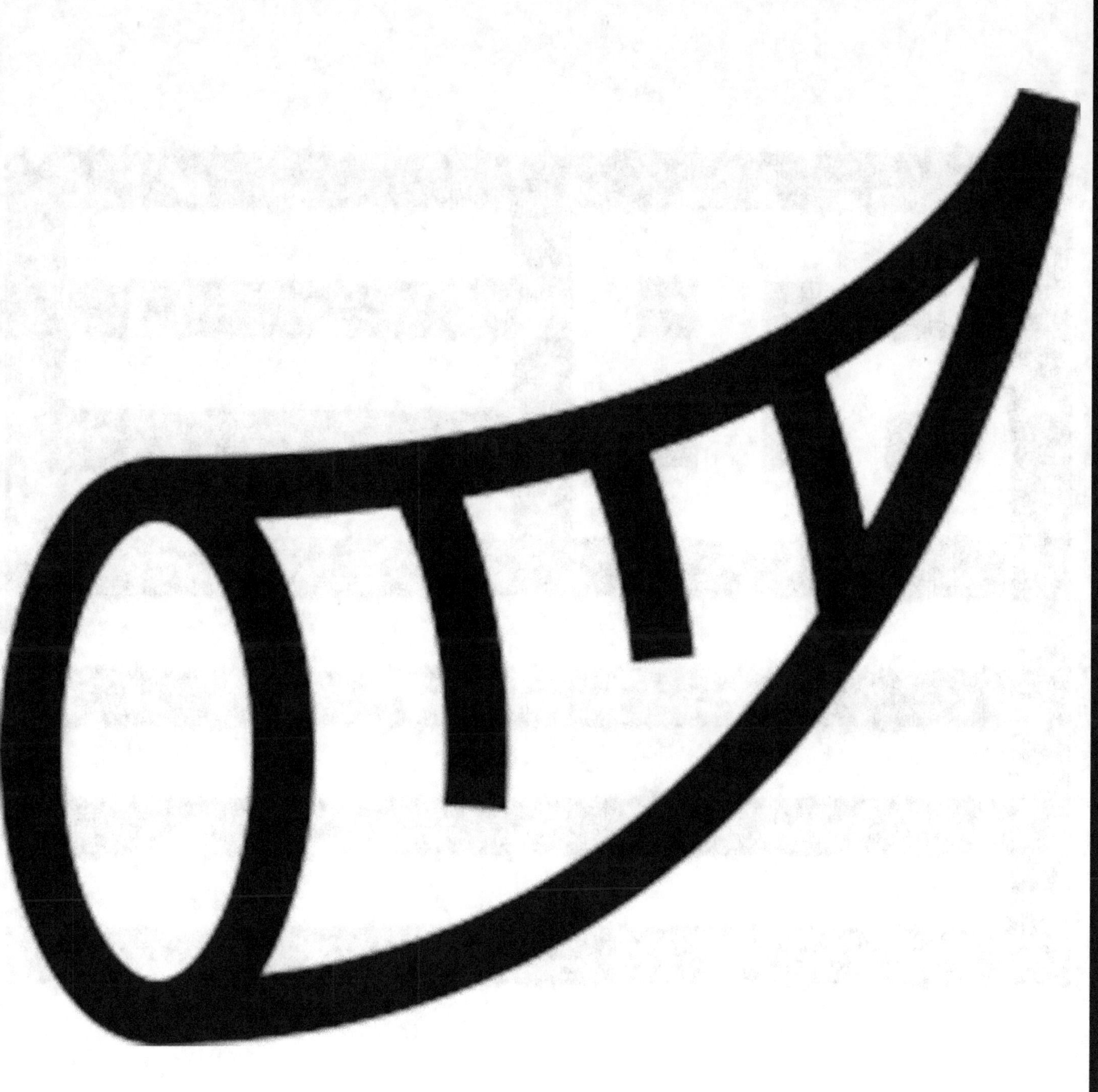

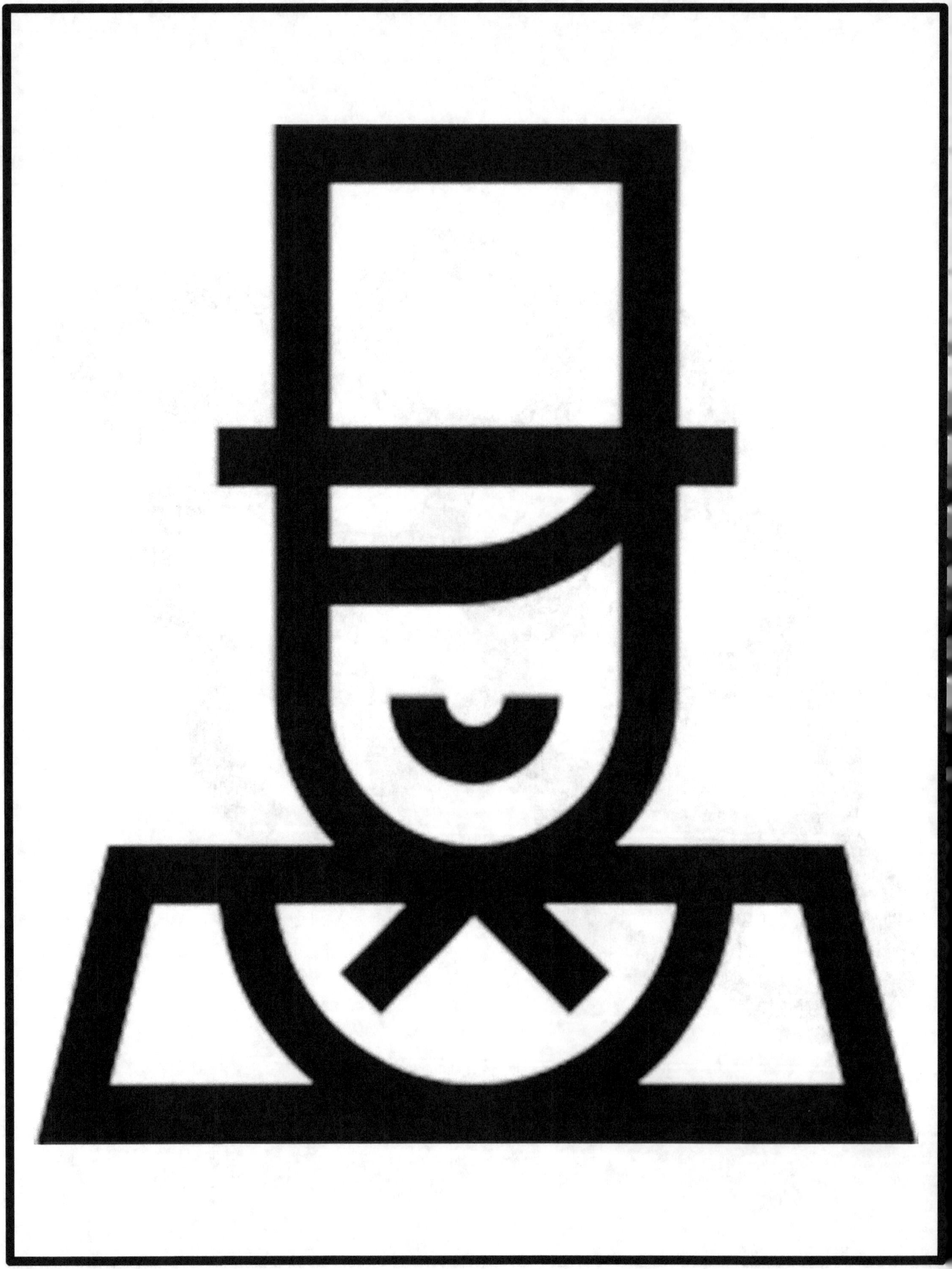

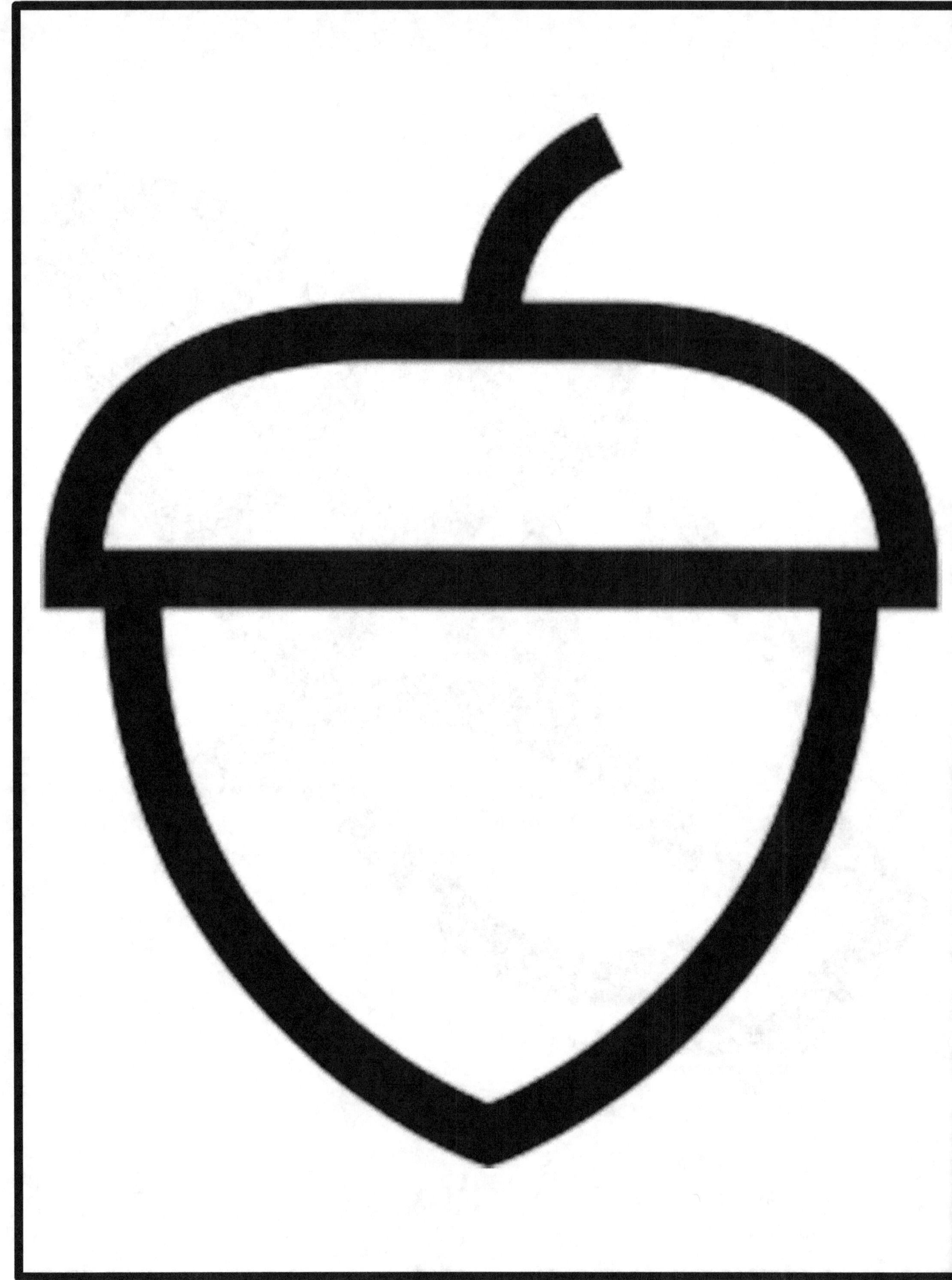

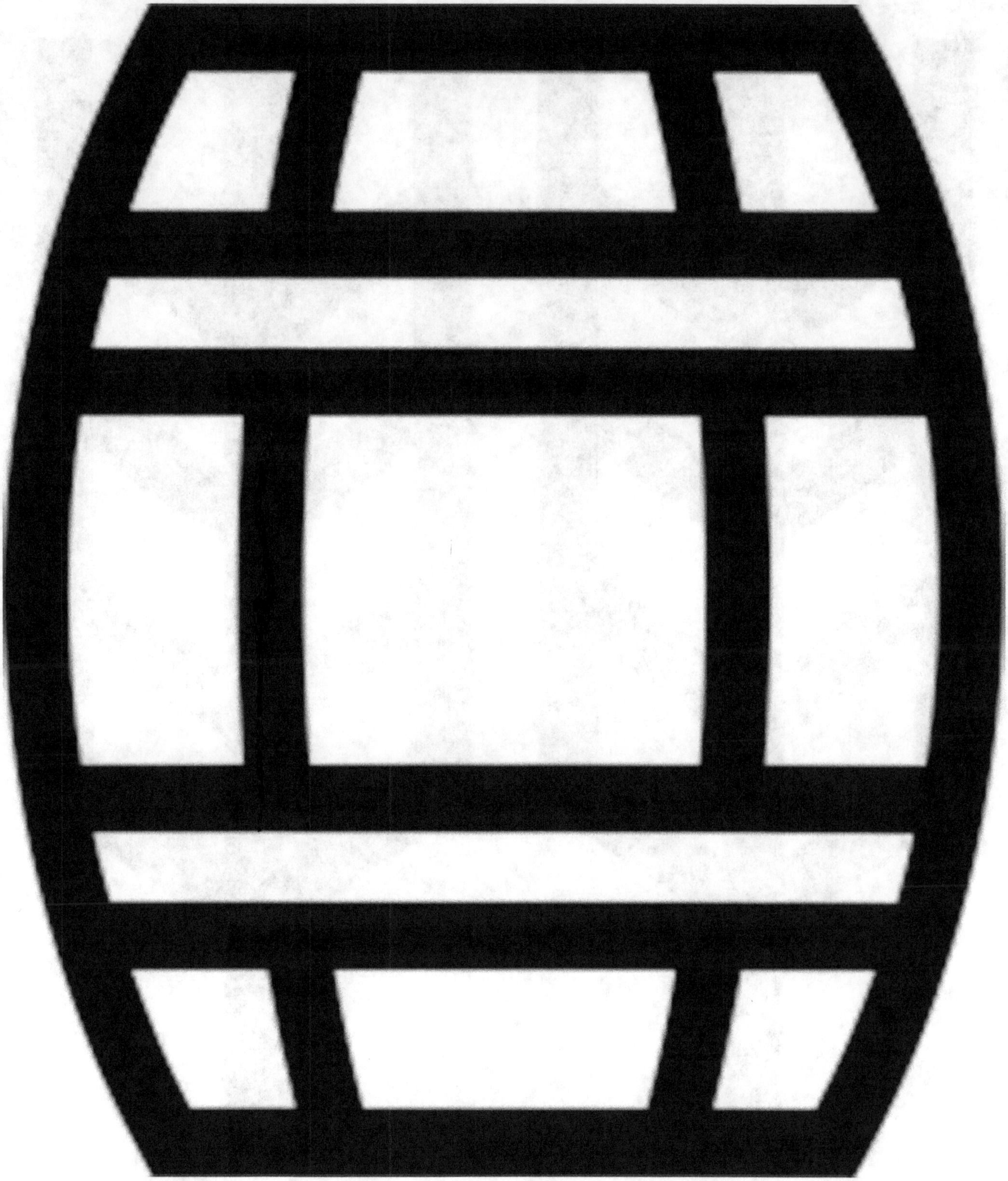